CW01637958

To serve, to strive and not to yield.
("Outward Bound" motto)

PSYCHIC PRESS LTD

23 Great Queen Street
London WC2B 5BB

ISBN 0 85384 052 0

This edition 1979

Photoset by Bristol Typesetting Co Ltd,
Barton Manor, St Philips, Bristol

GATEWAY

Contents

Introduction By Paul Beard and the Rev. G. S. Whitby 7

Chapter

1	Early days	12
2	Talking by telepathy	20
3	The influence of English lakeland	35
4	Learning and growing	41
5	Reincarnation	54
6	During sleep	63
7	A group of souls	68
8	The total self	80
9	Postlude	94

INTRODUCTION

GATEWAY is the record of a complex journey, part of which took place in early years in the English Lake District, but which ranges far elsewhere. It encompasses the whole of a short life, but it does not end with the tragedy which interrupted it. For all closely concerned, the tragedy, though exacting a heavy price, later turned into joy and fulfilment.

What this book largely tells is part of Roger's journey after death, though it is in no wise the product of professional mediumship. It is a more intimate document. Many feel for a while the invisible presence of those they have lost. To others it is an impossible fantasy, to be dismissed at once by the rational mind.

Roger's mother, over a course of years, found this sense of presence developing into a telepathic rapport which enabled her to record many vivid impressions of his continuing feelings and thoughts, and to pass on something of the enlarging spiritual philosophy he has begun to master.

"Whom the gods love die young," and perhaps through the retention after death of his young and flexible mind, he has been enabled to make a contribution of distinctive value thereby.

It need not be thought that Florence ("Tim") Whitby's telepathic sensitivity is some mysterious faculty debarred to ordinary people and therefore suspect. It is more inwardly attuned and more disciplined than impatient folk are likely to cultivate. But this book, thanks to Roger's descriptions of the process and the qualities needed, may help many to develop it for themselves.

Roger shows how natural a process it is. It is best done, however, under the guidance of experienced people. It was made easier in this case by the very exceptional closeness when Roger was on earth between himself and his parents, particularly his father, his admiration for whom, as the book shows, has continued since his death.

Those who formed the small team through which this book has come about are all of wide experience in the psychical field, which is a complex one. George and Florence Whitby, both ministers of religion, are respectively president and chairman of the Unitarian Society for Psychical Studies, of which George Whitby was the founder. He is co-editor of, and contributor to *Life, Death and Psychical Research* published under the auspices of the Churches' Fellowship for Psychical and Spiritual Studies.

Paul Beard is president of the College of Psychic Studies and author of *Survival of Death*, to which Rev Leslie Weatherhead contributed an introduction. He and George are long-standing members of the Society for Psychical Research. All three are united by close friendship and by a common bond of sustained love for the English Lake District.

Roger had begun to learn very soon after death how to communicate. Ten years later Paul Beard came to feel that Roger, now very well adjusted to his new life, had things to say which others may find of value, and that this could be brought out by a series of questions from his father and from Paul Beard which Roger would then try to answer by telepathic messages through Florence.

Later Roger declared that he had himself first imparted this suggestion by telepathy; thus it was he who had conceived the project and then carried it out with the help of those still on earth.

The results lie in this book, and provide a selection of topics, upon which each reader will wish to form, and is invited to form, his own judgement. Where selection has been made, the editors have been scrupulous in every instance to preserve as carefully as possible Roger's own meaning.

P.B.

* * *

Roger Whitby, born in 1941, was educated at Oundle School, gaining a School Leaving Exhibition, and at Sheffield University. His "Outward Bound" course at Ullswater included the climbing of Napes Needle. In 1962 he was awarded the Mayberry Memorial Shield by the University Engineering Society for the best student paper of the year, his subject being "Aqua-Lung Diving." He graduated with Honours in Civil Engineering in 1963. Two months later he was drowned whilst skin diving off Corsica.

Roger was essentially an "all-rounder." His varied achievements were due far more to prodigious and sustained effort than to natural facility, albeit he was blessed with the saving graces of humour and sheer fun. His self-effacing modesty tended to mask well-tested qualities of leadership.

His deep and abiding love for the members of his family was balanced by a particularly friendly and out-going nature that compassed folk of all walks of life. Where help was needed his response was immediate. Although markedly courageous and venturesome, those who knew him best recognised that his outstanding characteristic was his sensitive and loving heart.

In the eyes of most he was a very ordinary person and not lacking in human error, but this his worthwhile qualities carried with ease. Into his short life he packed more than do many who live to a great old age. For his intimates, rich and joyous memory will always "hold the door."

Key to the printed text: All questions addressed to Roger are in italics.

In receiving Roger's answers telepathically, his mother noted that Roger was placing emphasis on certain words and phrases. These are in italics in the printed text. This has been considered necessary because Roger's answers are usually so terse and concise that the points he emphasises make for easier reading and understanding.

G.S.W.

Chapter 1

EARLY DAYS

HOW did you fare immediately after your death?

At first I needed all the love and comfort I was given by my family and friends, who answered my need to get back to you. We had been severed too suddenly; our suffering could only be helped by certainty of contact. Then wise ones helped me enlarge, and integrate by their guidance. They gave me just enough help to set me on my feet again. Bonds grew here as well, and I began to see *our* place in the scheme of things. We go on together. Love got me through to you—not just my love.

The terrible cutting off from each other and the great need on both sides—this was a driving force. I was so near you all and couldn't help you see or feel me. The others here took a hand to help me, particularly Grandpa Holmes. He knew a lot more than I did, and he found out more. Then he set about trying to get through himself first. He did this with you, Pop, first—I think you "saw" me, didn't you? Then he "spoke" to Mum.

I take it that to some extent you "see" us? That you know our thoughts, feelings and deeds?

Yes. I see in varying clarity and I know your thoughts, feelings and deeds—not always in full but enough to be of help sometimes.

Communication is not possible without a driving force behind it. There must be this desire, force, impelling one. I had it. We were all reaching out. This is common to all who have loved and lost. Many other factors come in. Disbelief in communication on both sides is very inhibiting and often leads to rejection by one or both sides. If you persist and are prepared to experiment and investigate on both sides, you discover how really difficult it can be. Many are misled into experimenting in ways or methods ill suited to them. Others are not.

The more direct, simpler ones often find the essential channel which establishes a contact. Then they too can go astray in the way they use it—indiscriminately and gullibly. It's a subtle delicate thing which needs a very gentle handling.

I myself, learning here that communication was possible needed so desperately to tell my folks I still lived, but found, even with fine help and guidance, that I could not handle my expanded consciousness well enough—I flooded them with it—when we were all grieving so sorely.

Then I found quite early I could contact Mum's mind when she was quiet. This was the lesson I had to learn. It took me a very long time to learn it. All we needed was the faith which certainly was strengthened by investigation but also the quiet—the stillness of *cosmic silence.*

Have you profited in any way by dying with a mind full of youthful zest? Have you gained by dying young?

In my case I think I did, but that's not universally true. I learnt more from the suffering/separation. It took time for the zest, as you put it, to take over and help. The agony overlaid the zest. Wiser, older, tireder ones can be more able to profit earlier than I was. But I learnt, remember, from the suffering too. Most young people have suffering, unless it has been for them a genuine release.

Are people who had a very long life on earth likely to be slower in sloughing off the unwanted parts of themselves after death than persons who died young? My father died aged 92 in 1953. It is apparently taking him a long time to recognise his earth weaknesses, chiefly through being a very emphatic character. Dying young, your faults may not have had so much time to become ingrained.

This is a hard one, Paul, because so much is involved in it. It's definitely *not* a matter of distinction between old and young. Earth habits are difficult to slough off, and this is as true of the young as of the old. It most largely depends on a level or quality of mind and consciousness that you bring over.

I was luckier than one born in 1861 because having been at a modern university studying on the scientific side and with my completely free religious background, I came over remarkably open to development here. It is true I'd no entrenched position on earth, but in my own way was quite emphatic. Both those things helped me here, oddly enough, or perhaps it's not so odd, as all that goes to make up an emphatic character is very much needed here once you've really broken through to the real quality and purpose of consciousness.

This is the difficult thing—the really difficult thing to grasp. Even here with all the obvious aids we have and all the proofs we have, folk *will* imprison themselves in forms and images which they really don't need. But it's understandable. Pop used to say self-discipline was helped by removing gradually the "walls" of discipline erected by others to train their young.

It's rather like that here. We can be too free and wander and range too indiscriminately. Those who accept discipline can sometimes hold on to its forms too long. It's a question of having faith in what self-discipline has done for one and letting go the restraints earlier accepted.

Will you give a picture of your daily life and its activities?

There you go again, Paul—*forms*. People here live on very different levels. If you want to create a cosy life for yourself, in a beautiful house with a lovely view, you can. If you want to explore all kinds of interests you can. I haven't got a daily life in the sense of earth. When wanted I can be with our family—as they were and are. We come together in response to each other. They too pursue their course—in touch with some I am not in touch with. Common bonds draw us together.

At other times we are all pursuing different ploys. I am interested in many things. It is all caught up together in exploring the universe and the possibility of increasing contact and communication between the various parts and forms. Others have described, I believe, their lives here and their continuing earth forms. I am not like that. I *am* learning, I *am* guided, helped, instructed. I am disciplined and dedicated from *within*. I am a free soul.

What is your equivalent of sleep?

A pause, a rest, a floating of being, a letting go of whatever has been the search; letting the light and the music and the love of God come in.

It would seem that organs corresponding to physical ones exist. If organs of digestion and elimination are used at first, presumably this only happens as a result of fixed mental earth habits having not yet been shaken off?

Some newly come do not need or use bodily functions very much; others may use them for quite a time. All depends on how tied to the body one has been on earth. Some are really obsessed or possessed by their bodies. Others are not, are glad to be rid of them. But one has functioned so long in a body that some sort of frame is needed, and the one used to, familiar, is the best; it sets one free to forget a frame. No need to bother about adaptation to something utterly different.

When greater consciousness develops and greater powers are felt, body and functions just don't matter. In fact, there may even be times when high points of realisation, awareness, are being experienced, when the body, form, is not there. It feels like that; it would also seem that others don't see you then. You come back into their focus, as it were, later.

Are the organs that are not used by you equivalent to the male nipples of incarnates?

I think that's as good a way of saying it as any; e.g. I use my eyes and ears, but in such an extended or concentrated way as to give them super-functional powers—at times so super-functional that it might appear entirely different from their earthly use. When consciousness is added to so many of our activities here they are lifted into much greater dimension. This is what consciousness means and does. All right, the organs are there, but, yes, I think vestigial gets it most nearly.

They become vestigial and their original function is transformed into another form of consciousness?

Yes, the consciousness is the important development. On earth one isn't particularly conscious of functions which are operating well. Only when something malfunctions is one conscious that the organ is there. Here consciousness is what one experiences, i.e. extended powers of sight, sound, touch—the power of *knowing*, of *feeling, being aware.*

An interval clearly elapsed before you underwent your "judgement." What is your measure of duration, or is that now a meaningless term?

I'm not sure exactly, but I'd been through my main judgement when I was able to come through to you on holiday, through a lady who allowed me. Her wise one kept control, because after my judgement I was very distressed for you. I distressed her. She was a very fine person. She helped us all.

Was your teacher present at your judgement?

Oh yes, my tutor was there all right. You face it alone, but you need a friend; and I was glad of mine, my grandfather John. He's one of the wise ones, and I love him deeply.

Do we become different in appearance or shape?

Forms again! Yes, there are differences, but it is not so much shapes and forms we contact or communicate with at these different levels. The higher the level the more nebulous the form. Mum doesn't *see* me now, as a form—as a memory perhaps—but that is *not* me. All the same, we *are* in contact, and one learns this more and more.

Is there then a development towards formlessness?

Yes, it would appear so. All the same, some form seems necessary for most of us. It's an odd thing. You see someone you know, recognise them, make real contact and the deeper and richer the contact, the fainter the form after a while. I've gone on talking with Grandpa Holmes—*we've* gone on and he's not been there. But we still talked.

Telepathically?

Of course, both thought and emotion intertwined.

Chapter 2

TALKING BY TELEPATHY

WOULD it be wise to devise some difficult evidential tests?

Mum has a block about tests. Our "contact" is a spontaneous trigger. It sometimes comes off amazingly well and with complete accuracy. At other times I think it's slightly off at a tangent. When she's really "off" she's very, very off. She has strong feelings sometimes which can either help wondrously or the reverse. Usually we're completely *en rapport*. When we're not, we both know what to avoid. We may try tests eventually but not yet.

Can you give any hints of the modus operandi *of telepathy?*

Always the right mind "receiver" is needed, like wireless sets. When we try to communicate we act as agents who transmit or broadcast. But a mind on earth is needed to be the receiver. We concentrate on one. Others present may help if they are in tune. If they are not, they're a damned nuisance, and muddle the transmission.

You refer to folk on earth?

Yes, we have to be very careful here, and very clear. That's why the best evidence comes often in symbols and small signs. Long descriptions of anything are seldom completely accurate and we can't always be sure exactly what has got through. We know when transmission is going astray, but not how much. The light becomes more opaque, misty.

We can try to clear it and sometimes do, when the right word or meaning gets through. That's wonderful and we feel we've achieved something. At other times we're beaten and can't get a clear line. Once you find the best receiver mind it's wisest to stick to it; sometimes another mind picks up the true wavelength too. But they mustn't try to compete in a group; they must work peaceably together.

When you are about to make contact with Tim, what are the most handicapping things?

The only handicap is when she *doubts* me. Even when she is in distress, anger and physical pain I can meet her on a deep level. Surface disturbance makes it hard for her, but as long as she does not *doubt* I can get through. She has certain blocks born of doubt and distaste. On important things we are pretty reliable I think. The best preparation is a quiet place, a stilled mind, tranquil emotions, and a simple, straight humility, empty as far as possible of the ever intrusive self-important self.

Are there any differences, essential or peripheral, between telepathy with the dead, and telepathy between persons on earth?

Incarnates first. There has to be an affinity. Even if it isn't recognised it is there. In some it is clearly recognised and accepted as coming from outside. Others receive, but think it is part of themselves and their own thinking when it isn't. Its movement is quite independent of what you call space or distance. It's a movement which sparks off a response which you call reception.

An important element is acceptance for what it is. This recognition and acceptance seem to be very, very important. But it needs care and integrity. A lot of people are not honest about it or are rather silly. The real thing with honest people is *very* real. It must be accepted in order to develop and it mustn't be exploited. It's odd how it seems to have an independence and decision of its own. It puzzles us sometimes. We accept this independence and decision. We have to.

Now, *between incarnates and discarnates*. Here there often seems to be more control. Affinity and acceptance are still very important, particularly in the incarnate partner. The discarnate however seems to have more power in starting the movement necessary. Then by sheer force of concentration and will the movement can be sustained deliberately, sometimes for a very short time only and at others, as for example now, for longer periods.

Our powers when discarnate are greater than yours. We can initiate more easily and sustain the movement of our thought and will. You can tire in a way we don't. But you can learn to focus more by conscious training and effort. It is much harder for you. All the same I can always tell when movement is weakening and you are tiring. It's like the heart graph on the screen.

You are right to be wary and critical *afterwards*. When symbols are used they must have real point. We try to help you get the point ultimately—not always easy.

Between discarnates. This is very much easier, particularly on ordinary daily level. When it comes to perception in depth and spiritual training, contact between mind and mind is harder, and depends on so many other factors—development to date, willingness to learn, humility, and charity in depth and one's deepest needs, whether known or unknown, recognised or only faintly perceived. The essential movement of *mind* contact is the same throughout. The difficulties are the main difference. Your mind is influenced more by the denser matter of your brain.

On self-analysis I thought I caught myself thinking without words or pictures, i.e. imageless.

This is *exactly* what telepathy is, Pop. *Thought movement like a graph on a screen* you interpret and understand.

When you "see" or apprehend G's or T's "thoughts, feelings and deeds to some extent," do you see them as they actually are expressed on earth or in some deeper way?

Apprehend is the wiser word. We don't separate so much here, we see and feel and understand of a piece, as it were. As I *see*, sometimes I also understand more deeply than I would have on earth, but more usually, I understand, i.e. get a thought and through the thought I see. I do not see altogether clairvoyantly, but rather as one sees an expression or action reflecting the mind's thought or intention.

It's hard to explain. It's often so instant, quick, but contains much more than *instant* meaning; meaning that reveals much that has gone before leading up to that *instant* and also the possible future development. This contains something like your precognition. Can you work that out?

The operative factors in communication seem to be a partial sharing of consciousness at a particular level, and our own desire to share. The detached observations of psychic researchers tend to prevent communication except at the most matter-of-fact level, and often even at that. Is this indeed a gap which researchers and sceptics themselves make?

Researchers, by their very research, give us a line as it were. We *can* get through even with the sceptic at times. It's when they lose the thread of real *search* and become inimical that they break the thread and we are blocked out. Some of us still persist, but it's usually profitless. Research is a two-way thing; and the best results are a breakthrough on both sides, usually on a high surge and peak of sustained and shared consciousness. They think it's all due to their effort of experiment, insight and lucky guesses. But it isn't. We *share* in it all.

It is a group effort here. I'm seldom alone in our contacts. Many are interested here—some on the fringe, others quite closely concerned. Those on the fringe may go off to their own folk on their own ploys eventually. Don't imagine we are just one or two or three. Like the pebble we're having quite an impact. It's quite something to open up, keep open, and widen a channel. I *like* this continuing *flow*.

Can you offer any help on how to deepen the work of sensitives?

If they are not "God conscious" to begin with, then, yes, they need man's training to enable them to realise their real function as gifted, chosen and *potentially selfless* servants. A good parson-philosopher like Pop could do it better than any psychologist; you need a dedicated, religious approach, but also a self-critical and very much aware mind. It's a tall order for anyone.

What practical difficulties do you and others have to overcome when communicating?

(1) The first essential is a *peaceful* body, without undue strain or weariness. A tired body affects the whole nervous and mental systems. There must be ease and repose in the body.

(2) The mind must be equally at peace and as serene as possible. A troubled or disturbed mind will obtrude more—it cannot help it. Different people have different ways of gaining this peace. Music can help, or a favourite picture. Others can make their minds go still by thinking of some object; they usually discover this for themselves. Mum thinks of me in various earlier situations and the love wells up in us both.

(3) The emotions must not be dead, but they must be still, in the way deep water is still, and like deep water they reflect the warmth of the sun and the clarity of light. Coldness of heart is the greatest enemy and the biggest barrier.

There is all the difference in the world between a cool and clear mind and a cold heart. A cool mind is not a cold one: it is still and open. A cold heart is like granite to penetrate. A cool mind allows flow: a cold heart freezes.

We can and do influence coldness of heart, but it

is very difficult. That's why so many intellectuals who try to test for results get so little from us. So: a body serene, a mind open and clear and a warm heart.

Other helpful aids are well known and beloved surroundings for us, or a beloved possession held in the hands or near.

(4) Motive is very important too. Motives are always a bit mixed, and some not particularly lofty. But as long as they are warmly human and not entirely self-centred or acquisitive, jealous or too dominatingly exclusive, we can make contact. Selfishness, bitterness, anger, dominant ideas, make it difficult for us always to get over the complete idea or answer.

Sometimes the forms in which people think prevent us, and you get not our answers entirely, but our attempts to convey ideas expressed in their forms. We all have our preconceptions and they influence us all. That is why I keep much of what I have to say to the general and not the closely defined. In any event, I can only give you what I know or have discovered. Others may communicate their ideas clothed in different images: I try to be as simple and direct as possible and not to impose my images. People must choose their own forms and images to clothe their ideas.

(5) Harmony. There *must* be harmony on your side. Clashes of ideas and motives are inimical. That's why I could get through well when the three of you were together last. Paul accepts me as a friend, as I him. And you two are always open and warm.

(6) Sometimes it's hard to answer a call. That's why regularity and preparation are as important and valuable to us as to you. We can respond to an urgent call from you, and we do, but preparation is better. We too can be involved and committed in our work here and it's not always easy to switch. That's why sometimes others come.

Do you have temporarily to diminish your consciousness?

My consciousness is not so much diminished as concentrated, as it were, onto a narrower channel. It's quite a feat really and not easy. It's not truly diminution, but a temporary and willing use of concentrated effort on what might appear or be described as a very limited field.

There is a climate of opinion amongst folk interested in psychical studies that you folk have to lower your "vibrations" and in consequence become hazy, sometimes forgetting what it was you wanted to say, or putting it over wrongly.

It's all a matter of consciousness and ability to handle it, even manipulate it. Some are able here so to use their mental powers that they can make objects move, violently or otherwise. They can also temporarily appear themselves. It is all a manipulation of matter by the power of mind—on both sides. Where trance is involved there is co-operation from the living too and a willing co-operation. It is not easy to develop or achieve and it has to be handled scrupulously.

Desire and determination can sometimes outrun discretion and wisdom, both here and there. Many on your side who strive to manipulate matter deliberately and seek to experience escape from their bodies have to be watched and guided very carefully. It's a very subtle and delicate operation. We are all free agents and no one, either here or there, can control absolutely for all time, or be sure, entirely sure, of the ultimate outcome. There's always this element of tangential process.

I am saying that it is basically a control of consciousness—it is of the mind. Your mind has to operate within and upon your matter, but it is not the prisoner of your matter. It can become free of it at times and operate freely. We are free of it here and we actually communicate with and operate on your people best the more we remain free.

If we become enmeshed, as it were, in your matter then I think we are unclear, befogged as you say. Mum's mind is free at the moment. She's *with* us. We are touching and sparking quite spontaneously. This can be achieved as we are doing now, but it can also be something which spontaneously happens without apparent effort or aim on your side. Getting enmeshed is not easy to avoid at times. So much depends on your side and we can't control that if you are to remain freely operational.

Meditation, meditation and more meditation. That's how on your side you *free* your mind. Don't tie it too much to *forms*. Let your minds go free.

Training of sensitives to better standards is a so far insoluble problem. Can you help?

Like so many other things it rests with the quality of the individual. Where the emphasis of the present is on doing and not being, it is hard to grasp the importance of real consciousness. Anyone who realises fully that importance can safely train their own gifts. The real training should be to help them understand the importance of their own heightened awareness both for themselves and for others, and that isn't easy.

It really does demand a dedication and selflessness way beyond any average man or woman. It really is a matter of quite conscious and deliberate discipline and limitations; e.g., earlier Mum wanted so much to *see*; actually she's far better listening and *thinking* with me. This has come more as she willingly let go of all the earlier reaching out.

Now that you are an accomplished communicator, do you need others in your world to help you?

It depends. There has to be a real community of interest, affection, purpose, for other discarnates to be of help. They help most in backing up, as it were, helping you to keep your focus. I am asked to back up too quite often—and I do. Some back up out of curiosity and interest. The greatest help in focusing keenly comes from those who *feel* the most and are closely involved but also disinterested.

There is often said to be a good deal of team work behind the scenes, not normally apparent during communication. Would there be engineers, messengers, persons acting as transformers of consciousness, guardians, people adjusting wavelengths (as sound engineers do when music is being recorded)?

It depends on what you're doing; e.g. my contact with Mum is personal now; she and I only need each other now. When a bigger effort is being made by some on earth, e.g. experiments, TV programmes, healing sessions, then, of course, many more line up here. I've been present with others in many parts of the earth to help, to learn, to back up. As on earth, your interests and involvements line you up with each other, and you embark on this interpenetration exercise. Sometimes it's your own particular more personal group that embarks. At other times you're called in as it were.

When you say "line you up" I take it you mean in terms of your special and particular skills?

Of course. Special skills are involved much as on earth; e.g. I have a smattering of all kinds of technical know how, but others are much more able—knowing the electronics, magnetism, mathematical formulae, etc., of earth which they used and understood in earth terms. They, knowing all this, now try to co-operate from their increasing depth knowledge here to achieve their particular breakthrough. But this again is a matter of interpenetrating consciousness—and the interpenetration is a two-way traffic. The really open mind, best described for our purpose as the non-material mind, is the one our folk can co-operate with best.

Grandpa has a very keen power of focus at times—he learnt it before I did. He's the best backer I've got. Other discarnates who can't come through directly will use those who can. They may be unable themselves to focus clearly enough, but they can transmit and back up.

Let me just say—I had to learn by learning. I didn't understand enough about consciousness at the beginning. I was thinking too much in terms of earth, too mechanically.

The real contact is between mind and mind and heart and heart. You were on to the real help of the glass and alphabet as a means to focus your mind, as you say, to make yourself a centre of focused thought as you do in meditation. You focused your mind on the glass and alphabet and that pushed out intruding thoughts. It's an aid—that's all. In the same way it helped me for a time.

But Grandpa Holmes got through without anything, didn't he? And in the circle Grandpa "took over" one of the members and was able to speak through him, once this member really accepted Grandpa in his mind. This circle had helped you to a degree, but it also held you back; too distracting, too many differing thoughts. You did better when there were just the two of you completely at one—in Scotland and later.

All the time Mum was really my contact and she was learning steadily how to trust her feelings and perceptions. She's much better when you, Pop, are there, you and she work very well together. You really do make a unity; your clashes are quite, quite superficial. You *do* belong together and me too. Other mediums who told you to dispense with the glass and alphabet were quite right, but they didn't understand you had to do it your own way in your own time. And you did find it good to share—that really was important.

Now you know you share without anything showing—that's what I mean by external mechanical aids. It's a mistake that so many are making on earth. The real investigation should be into the nature of man's consciousness and the consciousness of all things. The cosmic silence is what you experience away from noises—(not music) from voices, from *things*. It's a living, pulsating silence—

so alive you want to sing for joy and dance. You do this, Mum, and so does Pop when he goes out to look at the stars. You've both got it—you both enter it. You both know what I mean. That is *real*.

Chapter 3

THE INFLUENCE OF ENGLISH LAKELAND

WHAT did the English Lake District bring to you and mean to you?

I first went when to travel that distance on a train was an excitement and an experience opening onto new worlds. (He was six years of age.) It was just the two of us, Daddy and I, sharing this growing world together. Then our walks and climbs together, with spring in our step and the sky in our eyes, and the earth and grass under our feet—the sheer joy of life, the *sharing* of it all, all the greatness and wonder and mystery of the *greater* of which our sharing was just a part.

All this stayed with me as I grew. It was the sharing that was the most important, and always it grew and grew, so much so that I had always the drive to share it with others—scouts at Westbourne Prep School and at Oundle School, and then with Ilse.* Ilse felt the same and it fused the bond between us.

* He tested out his German girl friend by walking her on the fells.

Colour and sounds became more and more vivid in my experience; and the strength of my own body, even when it wearied, merged with the rocks and the scudding clouds, the rain and the wind, buffeting and freezing. It was an exhilarating glory, repeated for me, here and now, again and again, as consciousness and awareness grows of this great *mind/cosmos*.

The Lakes were and are for me a gateway to what we call heaven—always we need our own gateway. The vistas come after. There were other gateways later, but none finer than those my father first took me through, and the sharing was and is the point of light at the heart of the vision.

When you were 16 you climbed Napes Needle on Great Gable in your stockinged feet. Can you say how you felt during that climb?

It's difficult to explain how intensely one lives in such a short span of earth time. Each hold represented such a concentration of effort and will and vivid living and contained so much varied emotion in which fear was not absent, that one almost expected to have added at least a year to one's age. And the exhilaration mounted and fought with fear and caution. It's a good thing to know fear lest the sheer abandon of exhilaration takes over.

How did you feel when you reached the summit of the Needle?

Exhilaration. Relief too but a new sense of power and achievement.

Did these experiences of intensive climbs stand you in good stead later in your earth life and also on your present plane of being?

Without any doubt at all.

During the early days after death, did the Lakes fortify you in any way?

Oh yes, more than any other part of experience in my last incarnation. I loved Corsica, but it was to the Lakes I went for strength, and remembrance of all dearest to me when I needed comfort and the certainty that all that was dearest to me was eternal.

In what way are you in contact now with Lakeland scenery?

Directly when I choose.

Actually on the Fells?

Yes. Also through memory, vividly recalled, and also through sharing with others like Mum and Pop and Paul whenever they go.

Have these Lakeland experiences brought you something permanent (other than just memories) which you now possess as your own?

Yes. All experience is permanent: the more vivid, the more life-giving, the more permanent, i.e. as an intrinsic part of the self.

By "permanent" I take it you mean character and personality building?

Yes, the *self* and included in the self is all the *sharing* I am trying to convey.

Is there a kind of "club" of Lakeland enthusiasts where you now are?

Well, hardly; but the sharing is so real we don't really need a club—it's just there and you're never in any doubt when you meet each other.

Have you talked with any of the Lakeland poets and writers?

You know how labels become quite unimportant when you know your way around. Yes, I know them and I share with them. But they've so much more to encompass here, so much more to interpret, that they think of their Lakeland poetry, writings, as their kindergarten as it were. It's so hard to convey the enlargement one knows here. It's not been so much a talking as a sharing of their individual awareness. They are distinct selves—so we all are—as on earth but with the "plus" this side gives if one can take it. Now, like all of us, they have been concerned with further integration and enlargement of consciousness.

Pop taught me to have respect for each man's privacy. I can speak in general terms with a clear conscience about the Lakeland poets and writers, but I must not seek to give details of their lives here; that would be a trespass. I cannot invade the territory of another's self unless I am invited. The best communications of this particular kind, that is, concerning intimate personal matters here in the discarnate, as I understand it, are those which are sought and offered freely on both sides.

Not all here believe in this very difficult and delicate type of communicating. If discarnates want to express matters that are private to them they can and they sometimes find their own channel. If they don't wish to engage themselves in this then I cannot do it for them; first, because I could only be an interpreter and could mislead, and second, because I have no right to speak for them. I can speak of our general and shared experience, and that's as far as I'm entitled to go.

Is there any great difference in the spiritual stature of these writers compared to that of ordinary folk?

Spiritual stature is no man's preserve. Non-poets and non-musicians are able to respond where they may not be able to initiate or create, and this response is also a measure of their stature. In some spiritual gifts non-poets and non-musicians can be superior.

Chapter 4

LEARNING AND GROWING

WHAT surroundings, landscapes or home do you choose for youself at present?

Wide vistas, spacious "open plan," light, light and more light.

Do some lead the equivalent of lives of cloistered contemplation?

It's difficult to be cloistered here. But you are able to withdraw when you wish and as often as you wish. I find the need to do both. Even our wise ones enjoy drawing us to them most. No man is an island. I range widely with purpose in inner and outer worlds, but they merge constantly. It's difficult sometimes to define limits, particularly with your group.

From which companions of spiritual stature do you learn at present?

There are so many. One of my happiest is my last grandfather John, and musicians. But I also get wonderful enlargement from engineers, archaeologists, astronomers and folk who have loved greatly with courage, like old man Churchill even. There are so many strands together in one hand. I learn a lot too from my old Pop and Mum and my family here. They can love.

Do you get visits and teachings from beings from higher "levels"?

You seek them.

Do you?

Yes, frequently.

It is very hard for us on earth to conceive of causation without an element of time duration.

That is true. Growth is not an instant thing. It has its own extending process, otherwise it would be nonsense.

There's no space: there's consciousness and this consciousness communicates at many varied levels. This is the *heart* of the riches and the richness of what we call life. Even at the lowest level communicating consciousness is a wonderful richness, wealth, but at the highest level it is the transcending wonder and mystery that poets and mystics, saints and angels, know. God is in it participating, gaining increase of being himself.

How should one become a "total man" on earth?

No man is master of all, but he can have interest in all aspects of life. Balance is absolutely essential. Whilst on earth he rests on and lives in the animal kingdom and *must* do so. His heart must be open and great; his mind must be open and keen; his spirit must be free and range the universe.

Only consciousness can make reciprocal contact. I'm really saying there's no way round; no avoiding the continuing consciousness of the discarnate world; and its ability to make conscious contact.

Are boundaries of personality much more permeable and interpenetrable than most folk suppose?

The more highly developed the personality the more capable of perceptive and creative sharing. This sharing extends to all who are participating and creates larger concepts, and higher possibilities of consciousness. The personality grows in the merging, but it does *not* disappear. It *grows* and in growing with others becomes creatively greater.

Pop, do you remember swimming with me?

Very definitely (In what seemed to be a dream.)

That's it—free, easy, relaxed, happy, outgoing and infinitely *"healthy."* That's how thought can be and our interchange—communication—knowing—merging (as near as I can get it).

You seem to say that really there is nothing but consciousness, layer after layer, and that outer material things, there and here (including our bodies, there and here) are really only concretisations of individual and group consciousness at a particular level?

Exactly right.

Discarnate teachers often say the next world seems solid, which seems to support a Berkleyan view. Comments please?

Yes, consciousness is all-pervading: if you like, we are all part of the consciousness of God.

We explore in depth *here*—no need to go to earth. We have knowledge enough of earth to start us off here; and if we need more earth detail we can usually get it via earth consciousness of those living on earth.

Exploration here is exploration indeed, to the very limit of identical consciousness, i.e. merging your consciousness with the movement of sound and colour or "tissue"—becoming part of, entering in, until you feel you've lost your identity or merged—but you haven't really.

Consciousness is a state of the whole being, not as some think of the mind alone. It's a totality of body and mind and heart. Some can dance their way to this totality when their bodies express the reach of their minds and hearts. Others are able to dance with their minds, as it were, or their hearts. But to be adequate it must be a totality.

Discarnates have to talk to us as if time persists there, but also say it is absent or irrelevant. How does one step outside time, if this is what happens to discarnates?

We don't. We don't step out of anything. We rather become conscious of a greater dimension in which all things move, where we can see *before* and *after* merging as it were. We are not inhibited by what you call the pressure of time. We see a flow, not 1, 2, 3.

Early discarnates could, one supposes, continue to carry around with them their old sense of time, as an illusion?

Quite correct. But many arrive here already aware of the illusion and are able to adjust better to our experience of consciousness. Consciousness doesn't change radically—it grows and expands. Realisation of a greater dimension *can* be such a tremendous discovery which could appear like a leap, but one has usually been prepared quite gradually for it.

Far more people are aware than is often known, and time doesn't bother them. They're too concerned with real being—the natural ones who respond naturally, the natural poets of earth. They take quite easily to experienced being. It's what they have been seeking all the time—they just embrace it joyously. Thinking ones can be helped in sleep, but they don't find it difficult to accept once they're here. It exists and that is all there is to it.

Is this an open-ended experiment the reach of which neither you nor we can foresee?

It's open-ended. All ploys are. One can only see so far—and hope. The rest depends on many, many responses from many areas. We are not so much *told* here what to do, as inspired, challenged, with possibilities revealed as it were. Teaching in the usual sense is not the right word. It is very misleading, or can be. We can be shown, we can be caught up in another's grasp and vision, but we are not *taught* as I once understood that word. It's so much more an exchange and a sharing. Some here may still need and find directives, but as they advance they leave them behind. I'm giving you my experience and the experience of those I work with.

Is it possible to find out spiritual information from earlier civilisations which could help us know?

Vanished civilisations are very interesting and available for study and for any information sought by us—as on earth you have your pioneers and researchers. Spiritual lessons are there to be learnt too, but one never learns by proxy. It is the situation to hand which is the teacher: what is learnt depends on the learner. The lessons are there. The *vision* and the *grasp* may not be. More than scrutiny or mental registering is needed—that's the most elementary and very ordinary fact.

Is your greater dimension really more an altered state of consciousness than an altered intellectual concept?

No. Greater dimension is *expanded* consciousness, not *altered* consciousness. Consciousness is consciousness. This matter of forms. Catholics pray to saints and have images always before their eyes. Others have guides and Red Indians. Others have Christ and the teaching of people like Paul, the apostle, and the churches' leaders. Others again have ideas, conceptions which inspire. These are not divorced from people/teachers/leaders, but it is more the conceptions which inspire and lift their awareness.

It is all very wonderful and mysterious, and it really doesn't much matter about the clothing. It's what is inside the clothing which is important. I came here remarkably free, but open to all the infinite possibilities in this universe. I am not tied to any one form. I learn just the same and try to pass on to you what I can.

There are so many High Ones, their influence pervades. It isn't important to them to be identified; nor to us really, beyond a certain point. It's these *forms* again. You can't get away from your earth images, your earth experiences. I *have*.

Identity is unimportant. When you are grasping or coming near to grasping a truth it is that which is important. Those who help you are not expressing *themselves* primarily. They are reflecting what they have seen and come to know as truth, and they can do no other than transmit.

They don't give a damn about their status when the spirit of God moves deep within them. And neither do we. We respond and give thanks and go our way to live what we have learnt, to ponder more, to return for more. We may meet the same one or ones: we may not. Another may add the next brick. Honestly, this grading, this comparison is of earth—not of "heaven." I go as myself—*and* I am accepted as myself. What I learn they leave to me. When I learn they give me more and more and more.

Do your present limitations of consciousness show?

My limits are all that I don't know and know that I don't know. When I strive to know, then I know of my limitations. *But one does gradually overcome them*, and then your consciousness grows. It's only when you look *back* that you realise you *have* grown. Ability to carry out tasks—yes, of course there is inability at first, but you either learn or you don't choose to. If you learn, *you* grow. If you don't learn and don't do the job, you stay in the same place until you're ready to get on with it.

What are the methods used over there to overcome such difficulties?

You get on and do the job—you botch, you learn. You try again and keep on trying. You don't make a silk purse out of a sow's ear in five minutes. You try and try and try until you learn as you do on earth—it means often your head is bowed, you eat the dust *and like it.* Then you get up, cleanse yourself and go on a much wiser guy and a much humbler, bigger one. Evolving spirit combines so many seeming opposites—will, imagination, passion, *"qualities of dew and fire."* You're carried beyond any images or forms and range joyously free.

What about Masters who guide?

We decide, and sometimes make bad mistakes. This is all part of our freedom. Certainly the guidance is there if and when we want it or can take it. You may *know* what not to do and still do it. Even knowing is not enough. The test is having the wholeness to do the right thing. You can know and still not do.

Does the will reside in the mind, but this will is not always strong enough to overcome reluctances and encumbrances in the brain?

Will in the mind? All is consciousness and in that sense will is in the mind. The individual consciousness is limited by our own response. The individual, i.e. us, decide our own response which is where you could say our will comes in. Our consciousness can be much greater than our response or we can *know how* we should respond and still not do so. In that sense the brain does not limit us. But there are those who because their brain cannot register all they are capable of knowing consciously, can be forgiven inadequate responses.

The brain must not be blamed always for what appears a weak will. It's we ourselves who decide how much and how far we convert our apprehended consciousness into reality and action. It's all really a matter of growing our own soul. The conflict inside our own consciousness—mind—*can* be described as an exercise in will power, so in that sense will resides in the mind, not in the brain.

There's always a conflict in growth, in real growth. Being *willing* to see moral values is the important first step, then comes the conflict of acceptance and action. Too many hide behind what they call their inadequate brain, or lack of knowledge or training or propensity.

Those delicate intimations which we call intuition or sometimes conscience, do these arise from the mind prompting the brain?

All arise in the mind; the brain transmits. Consciousness is never completely a separate thing—there's always flow and intermingling in consciousness here and there. The law is our own growth in perceptive consciousness of our participation in this constant, ongoing, creative universe—it's an ever-flowing process of creation overcoming all kinds of difficulties and destructive odds.

Think of the struggles of each individual and you have some measure of the constant strife for understanding that there is in the whole universe. And you also get a glimpse of what the love of God means too, which leaves us free for this kind of strife—for ourselves and for Him.

By understanding I take it you are referring to the quest for truth in its widest and deepest sense and then putting it into practice?

Yes, of course—you can't, if you think about it, understand anything which isn't the truth. Error—the opposite of truth—is a failure in understanding.

I am very bothered about understanding being used to gain mastery over others, a dreadful fact of history, anthropology, and particularly of our present time, here on earth.

That sort of mastery, that is, over others, is completely and utterly destructive. Milton showed us this in Lucifer. That is *not* mastery. It is wanton self-destruction and carries a terrible price.

In discarnate life our natures cannot be concealed and are they necessarily open to all others?

Our privacy depends very much on ourselves. Some want it, a lot don't. In any event the "nosey parkers" here or there don't really get anywhere. Minding your own business is one of the first real lessons anybody here worth anything learns.

You've enough to do minding your own business—that's the beginning of wisdom.

So much depends again on levels of perception. Just as on earth there are different levels—so here. The main difference is that here we're not so cluttered with material disguises, which on earth can and do often conceal the real person. The more perceptive over here, the wiser, the kinder and the tougher they are, and they're bigger too. That's why deception and pretence are pointless and you quickly realise that.

Can folk put on a false front on your level?

They can try, but it gets nowhere, which they realise pretty quickly. If they don't realise it they stay where they are.

Will mankind gradually add an extra dimension to its spiritual nature, with all the opportunities for use or misuse, which it will gradually learn to deal with?

This is completely true and by some already realised. Some realisation is quite conscious and understood; with others the realisation is not in the conscious mind, as you understand the conscious mind, but it is there none the less, and influences their decisions more than they know, sometimes by acceptance and sometimes by way of rejection.

Do you mean acceptance of good and rejection of bad?

Oh, no, it can be rejection of what they know is good but will not respond to. *But one doesn't stay on the same level* of consciousness all the time. Sustaining a high level is for the saints and high ones. We growing ones touch their perceptions and get enlightenment. I suppose ability to attain and sustain the highest levels is the point of the exercise, when we really see "face to face" and not "through a glass darkly."

Chapter 5

REINCARNATION

IS reincarnation true, as many say?

Reincarnation does exist and incarnations vary —I came over this time more complete than earlier. I was influenced powerfully by a finer element I'd left here. I needed this to learn much that I needed to learn. I'm not sure how much I shall carry into my next incarnation, nor how much say I shall have in it, though I think it will depend largely on my decision.

I think this is something I shall work out with others and with Pop. Our decisions, i.e. yours, Pop, and mine, appear to be very closely interconnected. We shall influence each other. I only know the next incarnation will be a hard and testing one.

The total soul is ever evolving. It is also free and can choose the point of incarnation. Therefore one cannot be dogmatic. A purgation may succeed where the previous incarnation failed, or it may *not*: in which case a different reincarnation must be chosen—before the total soul's present potential can be achieved.

To know the whole when incarnate would be too much even if it were possible. It's not possible here until far advanced. You can't demand a symphony from someone learning the notes. Each incarnation *can* learn and master some lesson; it can also reveal the need to learn others. Control and mastery in one part can lead to the need to master another control. A simple example is—with a greater mastery and understanding of a difficult problem or discipline, can come arrogance or impatience or contempt for lesser mortals, and pride is one of the greatest and hardest sins to be overcome.

We are literally so much one of another that saintliness is the only answer. "Bear ye one with another." The Greeks knew all about it—hubris—man as God. This lesson may have to be learnt over and over again alongside learning other lessons. Many evil men are so because of this.

Failures can be interrelated—in overcoming one you may fail somewhere else. You may succeed partially and put right something from the last incarnation. But you can also put it right here, and reincarnate to achieve a better integration or testing of earlier failures. You may have a sort of composite job to do in an incarnation—a welding of yourself, as it were. You may not succeed totally, but if you see clearly back here what is needed that's a big step forward.

Do we have a bank of both good and bad qualities which are not being fully expressed in one's present incarnation?

I'd hardly say there's a *bank* of anything. It's all much more complex and interrelated. We learn to mend and join slowly and firmly and then go on to make other strong bonds. You can't do this sort of division. There's little you can label completely *good* or *bad*. Nor can you split up consciousness in this way. You can't incarnate with part of a good quality and leave the rest behind. If you have learnt the value of being a follower of *truth* you don't incarnate with part of that value, as it were.

How you use your knowledge in a particular life on earth depends on you. You can allow circumstances to decide, or you can decide to change the circumstances. You can gain power and strength from your whole consciousness, from which you are never completely severed, or you can fail by allowing lesser considerations to deflect you. Your wholeness is your measure of success; and you decide. You don't have to be part here and part there—you *can* integrate.

What is necessary in a person's development before he can know of past lives?

Once you've adjusted, you assimilate and integrate your last earth life. That takes quite a time and includes judgement; judgement isn't easy: you can easily go wrong and be over-harsh with yourself. Your judgement has to achieve the right balance. This is difficult and delicate often, but when you are satisfied that you're near the truth, then it's safe to look at your earlier lives.

You are guided here by others and wiser ones, who help you choose the right time, but *you* choose. Then follows more integration and from that more choices. Decisions and choices here are as important as with you: the difference is, we can see implications of our choice more clearly. We may choose what appears a lesser way, but when we do we know it. We are not so blinded here by self-deception; though we can still be.

Such memories as I believe I have had tend to point to a moral lesson to be learned.

The important thing is what you have discovered and done now. If you have felt the need for expiation and have expressed it, that in itself is good, but the better part has been what you have actually done to serve others—for their sake, not your own.

We must already have many different contacts on your side.

Paul's needs are met; he does the asking and the seeking and he is answered. He is always helped by his teacher, but he has many anxious and able to direct him. They see to it he's put on the right road—but he makes his best discoveries by himself really. Some people are concerned with different group activities, but Paul's contacts are more with individuals from whom he learns. He wants to *understand* in depth, and he asks questions of many who are glad to meet his needs, and share their own work and investigations. When he seeks higher and deeper levels of consciousness the right help is given.

Different needs here are sometimes met by different leaders: at other times one leader can give help at different levels and does so when he judges it right. The training he's seeking and getting cannot be fully used on earth. He's training and being trained for much wider work.

Is a selection made of what to try to cope with in a forthcoming earth life? What principles of choice are involved?

There's always a guiding wisdom to help our choices, to help us put first things first, and to start on the bottom rungs. But we make the decision and we sometimes jump too high up the ladder and find we have to go back. A climb must be complete, you just can't leave out the foothills. You may try a few short cuts, but somewhere along the climb you have to meet and cope with difficulties you should have met earlier. They crop up later on as it were, and you have them to deal with additionally. So, if you have been wise enough to see and accept the right guidance, you ultimately achieve a pretty steady ascent without too many returns or ups and downs.

Are the only true fragments of former lives we are likely to remember those which have a moral lesson for our present life, and it is to assist *the latter that the memories are given to us?*

Deep moral issues come in a quite different context than in the former lives, although the basic issues may be and often are the same. Their resolution may take more than one incarnation. To remember them is no help. They must be recognised for what they are and when this happens—*then* may come some realisation that this has been a long-term task. Its completion may not finally be on earth. The final and complete absolution and resolution may and often does happen here. It's here that we really learn what "the peace that passeth understanding" means. Try not to divide off "here" and "there" too much.

It is often said that if we knew too much of our mistakes in earlier lives the burden of guilt would be too great to bear.

Growth in spiritual stature means an ability to accept and resolve guilt. Some guilt is quite unnecessary and irrelevant. Other guilt once accepted has its own redemptive power. All incarnations could be to some extent or other regarded as redemptive, in that all spiritual growth involves this element to a greater or lesser degree.

To know so little implies us still to be moral dwarfs.

Actually, you have your moral giants on your side as we have on ours. Knowledge itself is *not* the deciding factor.

Should not necessities of action, arising from former lives (what in the East is known as karma), like other spiritual facts, become part of the working tools given to man?

Yes, **part**, but it should not dominate. Spiritual growth has many many more avenues to discover.

Should karma always be regarded as opportunity, and not as a fate to lie down under?

The whole point of reincarnation is another *opportunity*.

In your world do you see the essence of a former whole incarnation, or just disparate memories?

You have choice in this: it depends how much and why you want to know. You can, if you are so disposed to make the effort, recall and see a life as clearly, if not more clearly, than you did in living it. On the other hand, if you only wish or need to know what you called the "essence," that too. It all depends on how deeply you need or want to penetrate. Often there isn't much point—it can be like playing nothing but scales when you've reached the Beethoven concerto. Alternatively, if there's something big you still have to resolve, then it is necessary to penetrate certain aspects of earlier lives really to understand what you're up against.

So you search back according to your present needs?

You can, yes. Some are more interested than others, just as a matter of interest—like the historian. Others do as you suggest—according to their present or immediate need. Or you may do both at different times. The historian's way is interesting, of course, but when you're interested in so much and there is so much to explore, your own smaller details don't seem all that important, at least not to me so far.

How far can one resolve the failures of an incarnation on your side?

As far as I can tell you, it appears that, as in all other things, we are as free as we want to be; some are influenced by others and their example to reincarnate, and vice versa. The choice is ultimately our own—even the influence. If the extent of the failure is fully seen, then it's just as hard to resolve it here as there—just as hard. This is no feather bed existence if you are sincerely pursuing the path of your own soul's pilgrimage. For some, it's easier to reincarnate. They find the limitations of your matter easier to cope with. But ultimately we've all to leave the limitations of your matter behind.

Chapter 6

DURING SLEEP

WHILST we are asleep, can we meet and share life with those who have gone before us?

Sleep is a very big question. The contacts exist and have all the varied ingredients of all human relationships—they vary according to need, or mood, or just plain being together, sharing.

Do you mean that much help may become openly assimilable whilst we are asleep, that there is such a thing as sleep-learning?

Much more is assimilated and learnt in sleep where such possibility is accepted and believed. Even without belief in such possibility, much help and knowledge can be conveyed. But where there is faith there is also more conscious co-operation and spontaneous flowering. A joyous meeting in sleep, for example, can mean healing and an increased capacity to tackle earth work which seemed too difficult before. But where the meeting is carried into waking consciousness, a new dimension is felt;

this can lead, does lead, and will lead to much finer insights, perceptions *and* achievements on earth. Conscious acceptance *is* important.

These talks have prospered. Would we have all discussed them together in sleep? Was the idea originated in the first place by you?

Yes, of course; we've cleared a lot of ground in sleep. We've needed to because of Mum's unhappiness; but she comes out of it when with us. She's doing well. I've always wanted to do more with my folks, and the time seemed ripe to tell you too. We go on steadily in hope and with quite a lot of well-grounded faith, i.e. based on the sound and the proven. You, Paul, came in quickly on cue—picked it up at once.

Ideas are elusive things—it's hard to tie them down always. They can be there in minds of several perhaps—rather vague and then the time appears when they come together. I think probably my wishes brought this ploy into the open, but you and others were always involved as it were.

Is sleep-learning just an extension of the process of the appearance of new ideas in creative minds on earth, so often seeming to them to come from outside themselves?

All learning is a flow and it's not easy to find its source. In sleep it is depth that is explored, and these depths can enter minds in depth and appear later, sometimes much later, as discoveries and new enlightenment. In sleep we are able to penetrate each other's consciousness very much more fully. Time doesn't come into it so much. We feel more at ease, more confident, more open. We are not at the mercy of externals so much; that's why so many better solutions can be found and are found, during and, as you say, after sleep—or "after sleeping on it." In sleep we go much deeper and are much more closely attuned.

What do we turn our attention to during sleep? Is it largely discarnate things or chiefly earth things?

This depends. You can grow just as much on earth as here—in fact you do. This is *one* world you know. If your point of growth is with you there, then you must tackle it there and in sleep you may be helped to do precisely that. It may mean we bring you here with us for a spell to let you "look down" on your problems as it were; all the same it's your own mind that perceives or doesn't perceive.

During sleep, how much less are we now than we shall be after death?

As less as I was on earth until I actually had the view of the Pyrenees at Perpignan outside my tent door. All the difference between a coloured postcard and the real thing.

How far is sleep experience less than the full *experience?*

It's the difference between a motor tour or a flying visit with high peaks of experience and a long stay which gets the real savour and full flavour, getting to know the corners and the crannies, able to "stand and stare" and go back to different sights and different sounds and colours.

Does the part of the self that is discarnate influence during sleep the incarnate part of the self?

Yes, it does; but the earth self is a free agent and can be wilful and blind and unco-operative. Influence in sleep is always a great potential, is always there. How much the potential is realised depends on our use of our waking lives. This is the test which we sometimes fail, sometimes pass. I didn't do so badly last time, but I had good help from Pop.

Perhaps I have overweighted the incarnate side. Just as often you, Pop, co-operate in sleep with the discarnate. You *express* yourself in sleep much more freely than you do on earth, but it does not *start* in sleep. In fact it is in sleep that you often are able to do your most valuable work—because you bring exactly the "down to earth" quality which some most need. But also in sleep you are lifted, inspired, which can help enormously in your earth life, but also adds by your response to our life here.

"Joy in heaven" needs your contribution too, just as much as ours. It all depends, you see, on *you*—*your* needs perhaps, *your* progress, *your* quality, *your* response. Just as I learnt so much from my parents on earth when I responded—so I've learnt from them here. It's a two-way traffic always. We take as well as give.

In other words, when we go over, shall we find a whole accumulation of acts we have performed during sleep in earth life but which almost add up, as it were, to a separate "sleep incarnation"?

You will find you take up threads of contact and communication with many who have found you their friend. You will find the sort of quick and spontaneous response which comes from shared experience, consciously remembered.

Chapter 7

A GROUP OF SOULS

CAN you remember where the earliest life in which you cared about music took place, and about when?

I began in Spain with a pipe, but became far more devoted to music in Greece, about 500 years, I think, before birth of Jesus. In Greece I played a kind of flute, a development of the pipe. I loved it. In every life I have had an instrument—a pipe, a flute, a clarinet, always wind instruments.

I played in the open air at all times, whenever I could; in the harbour to catch the sound of water against stone and wood and sand; and on the hills to sing with the wind and the birds and to catch the sound of light as it faded over the water and the land. The music travelled like a homing bird back to the nest. I used to feel I travelled back with it to my source.

What about singing? You were an undistinguished member of the Oundle choir, but you liked to "let rip."

Yes, I sang always. Never outstanding, but

adequate and it meant a great deal to me: a major part of my life—all music.

At what period were you a Greek?

Age of Pericles. Humble harbour worker, younger brother to Pop. Pop had the same job. We were both mentally very alert; took an active part in *Athenian* life. We worked at Piraeus. Practical politicians with a difference, *not* trade unions, we mattered and knew we did. It was a great life, one of the best.

When a long while ago I sensed you as wearing the robe of a Grecian philosopher, was this a convenient symbol of part of your essential self?

It's truer of Pop, Paul, but his mantle fell on me. Yet I am not he. I seek and search differently though we are very much alike in our seeking. We are *both* seekers of the truth and have been for a long, long time. Later, in the early 16th century, I was at Oxford for five years, and Pop was my professor of philosophy.

Pop has always been a solitary. He sees and feels so much more clearly and deeply than the average. He is a natural seeker, questioner, and he feels acutely. This has always made his responses quick; both physical and emotional response is often lightning quick; but at other times his emotions grow with his thoughts as they penetrate. Then it is that his sense of the beautiful, which has always been very marked, overflows.

Has George, as a philosopher, a long-term part to play in expressing a working concept for living sub specie aeternitatis?

He is the sort of leader we all go to at some point or other. He helps us all to see—*from the centre*—all those aspects which are affecting us, personally or as beings in a complex simplicity. He is not deflected by a new discovery or realisation. He fits it more in its proper place.

This means collaboration to a certain degree, but only insofar as it serves the whole vision. He responds to other men's ideas; he gives them their place. He is just and fair, not easily satisfied and not taken in.

He serves truth, and works well with all such. He is *just*, but will not pander. This means men like him are often solitary seekers, but they do work with others when understood. They need their like—men who examine and examine and give us real, balanced insights. These men seldom hit the spectacular or the headlines. They are still the men to go to for leadership.

You seem to suggest a group of souls comes together as the result of trial, error and experience, and can be added to, much as any close group might on earth.

A group of souls has a beginning. A central core stands steady, but it attracts and draws in kindred ones. Sometimes some hive off. They may return, they may forge far ahead of that group. Even then they can come back to teach, lift and carry part of the group with them. The group is never closed, static or set. It is a flowing, moving entity. No. Entity suggests a closed shop. A group is never that.

Is there another word or phrase you prefer?

"Being" is the nearest I can get. "Being" suggests the fluid, living, vital thing I want to convey. When you experience this intense group vitality and *see* it working intangibly in so many ways, you'll know what I mean. A simple example is decisions taken in a Scout court of honour which sent us out on our various ways and had important effects on our lives both in doing and being.

Some think of members of a group of souls as inherently belonging to the group?

Ultimately that *might* be true, but my experience so far is as I have described. Marco Polo ranged widely, but he remained a Venetian.

Is a further growth of consciousness needed before these relationships can be more fully realised?

This is where *group* integration comes in; and it can be just as hard as the personal sort. Growth of any kind is never easy here or there with you, but we do help each other in the hard work as we grow in consciousness both of ourselves, of each other, and the consciousness we come to share more and more. Bringing up *shared* consciousness to a higher common level, as it were, is hard work. I've still a lot to learn.

What limits are there in group work?

As on earth, limits between inner and outer action merge; it's not a clear line where inner decision becomes outer action. Similarly with shared consciousness. Group thinking can influence you as an individual, but you can choose then to act sometimes with the group, as a group, and at others as an individual, but in line with group thinking. Membership is something that grows naturally from the reality of this genuine, shared consciousness. It's all a matter of growth and experience.

What draws individuals to a particular group?

It's *something* that *happens*, and you know it unmistakably.

About how many might there be in your group at present, or as you know it at present?

Here we are twelve at present. Down with you are twelve more. Some you know. I mustn't say who. This is your sphere and you must be free. I mustn't mislead in any way. It's very easy to do so.

Your group could grow as can ours. It must be free flowing. We mustn't erect dams. If we do they can burst and this can cause a spiritual havoc we have to repair. It's better we don't have to do that kind of work.

The formation of a group is a long and very delicate operation. We're all learning all the time. The pattern overall is made up of many other patterns and it needs highly developed spiritual skills to use and merge them all into a clear unsullied light. All groups are in a state of becoming. That is something known and accepted as our glory. The more we accept that, the more we accept each other and other groups, the freer, the clearer, and the higher we go. It's exciting, exhilarating, it's stupendous and so enlarging we want to sing all over God's heaven.

Number has no bearing on quality. Number often decides work undertaken. There can also be co-operation between groups not only for work but also for development and education. Some smaller groups can undertake a special assignment, as it were, which can be both a difficult task and test. Part of a group may not succeed as well as the rest of a group; then they come together for self-examination and assessment before continuing or finishing the job.

There are different types and stages of judgement. You can have a group judgement here; something like you have on earth in, for example, a college committee. Here, out of this kind of judgement in a group grows a greater depth and unity of purpose, and a closer, stronger group is formed. Larger groups tend to be more wide ranging, but their quality can be just as high although different in expression.

Comparisons are not really possible, and not much help where the truth is sought and where love is the guide. There's too much comparing on earth although, even with you, wiser ones recognise the importance of motive. Where motives are of high quality, their expression is not important. Here we see the motive more easily and do not make your sort of harsh judgements.

This suggests a large area of mutual trial and error within the group, rather than the new or junior member of a team working on a particular project under close supervision.

There are always those, there and here, who want to be organised. If they need it, they are given the directions they need. Always the aim is towards self-reliance, self-knowledge, self-acceptance. We are all *free* spirits. What we choose is what we are. There is never any compulsion; only response, acceptance and dedication. There is constant reappraisal and judgement, whether alone with oneself or with others. Even those under rule or direction have this. Our teachers, leaders, wise ones, are not our judges, and there are no Hitlers here.

When we reincarnate, is it likely that many who belong to the same spiritual group would come back together, and therefore would find a kinship of task?

This is demonstrably true. You have good evidence of parallel incarnations like Pop and me and others you know. Not always do parallel incarnations reside in a family.

What is the real meaning of a family in the spiritual sense?

This is something that evolves and not in one incarnation. It can begin in an early incarnation and develop even when its members are not in the same physical family in later incarnations. It is closely allied to and part of the group development. The growth of the deep spiritual links in different incarnations can be advanced or retarded at different times, dependent upon the free human response to new circumstances and conditions. Sometimes the advance in spiritual bonds and understanding is deep and penetrating as members link on at deep levels to each other in their experience and responses.

In this incarnation our family has come a long way. Then our efforts at understanding, helping each other, carried us further. Our efforts to understand were great. Then out of our loss and suffering we gained an even greater sharing at depth and in height of vision. The channels opened to our spirits, and kept open, have been made clearer and surer by our fidelities to each other and to the truth and beauty of God.

Throughout we have been steadfast, despite periods of doubt and uncertainty. Pop is *Mr Standfast* and has helped Mum to hold on in her bad questioning times. I have also been helped by Pop enfolding me about him in all parts of his life. I come now and here (to my parents' home) and know how much of lovely memory there is around. We'd a great growing time together this time and it is going on.

What spiritual inferences can lie behind the bringing together in a family of souls who are inimical to one another, or largely so?

Strong differences in families can occur for many reasons, such as deliberate choices which bring about a feeling of not belonging in a spiritual sense to a particular earth family.

A choice or decision to reincarnate into a certain family may be made in acceptance of its future difficulties for a number of reasons also accepted and recognised clearly and fully. The ability to work out those difficulties will vary. Some develop the ability, others fold up on it and need to work out a solution another time or another way. Some work out the solution in the same life but not in the family.

Others who start well in a family can become inimical because wrong choices are made on deeply spiritual issues, which are denied by one or more in the family and accepted by another or others. The conflict is real and remains a conflict unless and *until the basic love relationship which all accepted initially* in varying degrees and at different levels is restored and reinstated.

This is seldom a once-for-all restoration—and means often a lifetime of varying tensions, in which much *can* be learnt. Sometimes it's not until earth death that perhaps the real lesson is learnt and the issue resolved; sometimes not even then. Tensions like this *can* mean a great step forward; complete failure is less frequent than supposed. But if failure there is, it's to be dealt with ultimately on all sides. Challenges to us all come in many guises; it's seeing through them which marks our growth and maturity.

Very often members of an already emerging group, incarnating in very different milieux, are drawn together and recognise their true affinity of purpose. They come together sometimes by the propulsion of their own impulses and instincts; at other times discarnate members of their group take a hand. It may even be that they never actually meet in the flesh, but, more often than not, they contact each other in thought forces or by interchange of ideas in activities they share or support or initiate.

Sometimes they come into conflict—or so it seems—but their conflict is always a creative process with a positive result. They never destroy each other. At a deep level they are always working together creatively. Where they are continents apart they are often working along parallel lines with similar aims and in very similar conditions. But where there is very little obvious similarity there is always in-depth compatibility of purpose. When they meet there is often instant response to each other, recognised or not.

Members of an emerging and developing group always have *some* affinity of spirit. They can and do meet others from an earlier historical period who lived under similar conditions. They may even have known each other, but not established any relationship of any significance. They may have worked together but with different aims. Their aims may continue to diverge or they may work out a more creative line together. The possibilities are legion.

I take it the individuality of the self is never lost in the group, identity does not disappear?

Never. This business of losing oneself to find oneself is often seriously misunderstood and the emphasis is put on the *losing* not the *finding*. In the *finding* we grow.

Groups are not mutually exclusive and much depends on your own free will and choices, both there and here. You *are* free souls. We all learn differently and take from each other what we can best assimilate. This varies from time to time. It's the value of being in a group. We can miss each other quite badly at times and may go off at a tangent—and then back we come to what I can only describe as a joyous homecoming, really having learnt how we each answer another's need. It's all part of completing a love pattern.

Chapter 8

THE TOTAL SELF

HOW far during sleep can we have access to what might be called the whole sum of ourselves, our total self?

Not often can you come anywhere near the sum. I can't be dogmatic about this. Most of us find it hard enough to come near it once we *are* here.

During sleep, what governs our having access to our total consciousness?

During sleep you are not so limited by your brain. Your *mind* can operate better and can often convey meaning and truth more clearly. But as I said before, you cannot in sleep attain your full mind.

I cannot understand why in sleep you cannot attain your full mind, unless something from the earthly incarnate consciousness is holding things back.

This knowledge of our "total self" or "total mind"—i.e. total to date—is *not*, repeat *not*, easily achieved even by discarnates who still find much to learn when they come here. In the process of learning to integrate with the part of the self that did not incarnate, they can also by learning add something, i.e. realise more of the potential of the part of the self that incarnated, during the integration process. Sleep is not continuous enough. It is true much *can* be done in sleep in integration and realisation which is of great benefit later. Much can be carried through to the incarnate consciousness. There are no short cuts. The job has still to be done here.

If the man incarnated on earth is only a fragment of his total being, the relationship between the part on earth and the discarnate part "left behind" is by no means clear.

The mind is always complete, so that whilst there are, as it were, different levels of the mind and consciousness here and there, there is never real separation. Sometimes the greater activity *can* be on the discarnate side; then the problem of integration later can be difficult. Usually, the greater activity is on the incarnate side, because that is where the real need to learn lies. But don't get the idea that the split, as it were, is always 50-50 or 75-25.

Sometimes what you might call a very large part of the total self incarnates, and does a really fine job, becoming finer still. At other times almost an elementary incarnation is made, because a very elementary lesson has to be learnt before real growth can proceed. You know yourself how some folk could be very fine indeed if they had only learnt a very elementary lesson, e.g. holding the tongue.

What steps did you take which brought about rejoining your part which did not incarnate this time? And have you met the spiritual leader of your group?

You don't take steps. Rather you experience enlargement. With each new adjustment and perception you regain those parts or elements of your portion of the self that did not incarnate, and which you can now absorb. In this you are helped by many. I told you my grandfather was my greatest helper at first. The others quite naturally, almost casually, help one's progress.

Then, one day, when you look back, you see you're a very much larger person than you were. In our group, as far as I've gone, there is no one leader. There are several wise ones who *may* know one high one who guides them. They don't say. I imagine they are like us—in contact with more than one leader. Understanding, knowing, perception, is so many-sided. We go where our need is best met.

I can find no empirical *evidence for a "larger self" on earth, and I get tough about hypotheses being trotted out* ex cathedra *as if they were established facts.*

Whatever such folk think they are talking about, Pop, they are only pointing to potentiality: here it is an actuality. They are not the same.

May I summarise my understanding of what you have been gradually trying to convey to us? We each have a total self which, on occasion and for a time, becomes complete in the discarnate world. This total self is usually and should be an ongoing, a growing and developing, entity. When incarnation takes place it is a part of the total self that incarnates. Hence the self is in two parts, one discarnate and the other incarnate. The incarnate part may not be consciously aware of the discarnate part, but the two parts are never sundered. Always the discarnate part seeks to influence the incarnate part, successfully or otherwise.

Sometimes the incarnate part is consciously aware of the discarnate part and its attempts to influence it. When the incarnate part becomes newly discarnate, in due course it seeks to join the part of the discarnate that has remained in the world beyond death. This joining and merging into a total self can prove difficult, because the part which was on earth has still a lot of growing to do, and also because the part it is now seeking to join can and should have developed further on its own meanwhile.

This gradual expansion of consciousness back to a total self formerly possessed cannot be a new state–though it might seem "new" in the immediate discarnate experiencing of it. Would it soon seem familiar again?

The odd thing is that it doesn't seem new at all until you consciously reassess yourself. As on earth, you tend to accept your own growth quite naturally, even automatically. It's when you look back, as it were, and recap. that you realise the immense expansion that has taken place and you sometimes marvel at your own compass.

When earth folk talk glibly of a higher self, they tend to speak of what in discarnate life is an actuality, and assume a possession of it which is not really theirs on earth; thus they take a seat higher up the table than they are entitled to. Is this what you are saying?

Exactly so. Again the odd thing is that those who talk so are not those who are using or incorporating the discarnate part of the self left in "the beyond," or making the best use of their earthly potential.

Can some on earth contact the discarnate part of their self without particularly being aware of it?

Some attain quite a high degree. They are not really very concerned about it. They achieve it often by the right decisions which set in motion the right channels of consciousness. Then it becomes like a flow, back and forth, without those who experience it on earth being consciously aware of what precisely is going on. As it were, they just get the ideas as such, and then evaluate them. What flows to them appears to them to have come from within themselves.

Some do draw consciously on their discarnate self and express it in their present incarnation, e.g.

Cardinal Heenan who has just come over. But you'd be surprised to find others who are doing this quite unaware of it. Some are very unusual even unacceptable types, folk who are not particularly concerned with the world of fact and appearance of fact.

I take it you refer to those who are not interested in material rewards, the so-called facts of life, as distinct from those who seek fact *here and on your side in the selfless pursuit of truth?*

Yes. Your quest for fact and their acceptance of what seem mundanely facts are poles apart.

Do folk on earth who are of very poor quality, really evil people, have a discarnate part of the self even now?

Yes, they have, it's their main hope of salvation. Of course, the discarnate part is in constant process of growth, and an evil life on earth diminishes always, so that the merging into a total self can be very long delayed. Some cannot merge without a long period of what you call purgation.

Are there very low levels on your side?

Low levels—yes—the levels of the unlearnt, failed ones.

You have spoken of the tough job of integration. What makes the toughness?

Sometimes an earth life has been very fine and integration flows in more easily, but at other times greed, power, selfishness come over so strongly that finer lessons learnt earlier are swamped. The integration is tough before a right assessment and balance are won. We are as good at kidding ourselves here as you are there; and we don't like the truth even when we see it and want to follow it.

When discarnates don't like the truth about themselves, or are otherwise being laggards, whilst acknowledging free will is theirs, who decides when spiritual pressures will descend on them?

Ultimately you decide. Pressures come from inside you, from the group, from teachers, even from the eyes of those you meet. You have to resolve it, sometimes in a wilderness on your own, sometimes from the one you go to. At other times it's something you share with several who are doing the same thing, but you're blind until you are ready inside. You can't go on sharing properly until you can clear that particular beam in your own eye.

How does the link operate between the part of the self on earth and the discarnate part?

If the mind did not remain complete you couldn't have growth in any continuous satisfactory sense. There would be too much fragmentation. The link between the discarnate part of the self and the part incarnate is this *willingness* to respond, the willingness of allowing depth to call to depth, of being prepared to let go of many things desired to achieve a finer purpose—to lose the world to find one's own soul.

I take it then that incarnates are never fully *conscious of the discarnate part of the self, but you can have intimations of it or of something coming from it?*

True, you can't grasp it all, but you certainly can be *aware* of it.

Does the earth part of the self when it is paying attention to, or listening to, the discarnate part have to get into a state of higher consciousness in order to receive, and at the same time dim down interference from the daily incarnate part?

This is so true: you know this from your own meditations, from all your seeking of God. Man seeks in so many ways. Ultimately it has got to be his own quiet entry into the cosmic silence.

If the discarnate part of the self experiences and learns, whilst its other part is on earth, then our consciousness would function at different levels simultaneously, at a fast level in the discarnate part and at a slow level in the earth part.

Pace hasn't a lot to do with it. It's more a matter

of quality. The quality incarnate *can* be very fine indeed. Usually, the incarnate is having a struggle which may seem to be slow. It really isn't a matter of time or pace. Can you get my meaning? Here, it is true, there does not seem the same hard struggle. Actually there can be enormous effort here which on earth would appear hard struggle, but here there is more poise, balance, equanimity.

Can the incarnate part of the self ever *be of higher quality than the discarnate part left behind?*

A great amount of quality *may* incarnate from the total self. The remaining part is not inferior in quality. It may just be different—in a sense not required.

In a sense, then, consciousness could be in two places at once?

Consciousness can and does operate on different levels and can function in what appear to be two different places at the same time. Your incarnate consciousness does exactly that. You don't need me to illustrate two levels—two different places. You know from your incarnate experience of telepathy, where you can be in one place and know what is happening elsewhere and even participate in the happening.

Other teaching suggests the twin-soul concept is real, that man was originally hermaphroditic, that the two parts split into male and female selves and will eventually become again as one.

I don't know enough about the origins; it's quite an attractive thesis that the original life cell was hermaphroditic. What I do know is that developing evolving consciousness is sexless. Quite seriously this is the eternal plan—a facet of the eternal, whatever else there may be. It's all such a baffling, exciting and stupendous experience—this evolvement of conscious being. You forget so much of yourself—or of the self that seems so important lower down. You're caught up in such a wonder, such a vibrating, pulsating spiral. I really can't describe it.

It's very tantalising because it's important we contribute ourselves in our own growth; and yet we have to learn the patience and integrity of a plant, of a seed, which can only grow when everything is right. The *right* time depends so much on what is within the plant, seed, and that certainly can't be hurried or changed. But growth can be helped by good external conditions, provided sometimes by others, sometimes in human cases by the absolutely *right* choice.

So often we want to be or try to be other than we are, whereas we have to learn to be patient with ourselves as we are, at a given time, and then make the best and truest choices. There really is often far too much over-reaching. I am being taught and guided along the lines of the free soul, which seems to be a very important element in the eternal plan.

The freedom appears eternal and as an essential ingredient in what you call, or is called, the Source of Being. The source itself would appear an eternal flow too, not something attained or held for evermore. Nothing is *static*, nothing is ever lost. Much is outgrown, extended, developed, refined, energised—but the free soul remains. I'm giving you my own experience—as far as I've gone. It is however not just *my* thought or reaction. I am learning and under guidance from many much higher and further along the road. Many may claim wisdom. The wise ones don't.

Marriage and sex would then often be a symbol, and imperfect expression of true union of the twins, and thus be both a disappointment and a hope.

Twin souls, unlike earthly twins, are not born. They grow. Many a marriage has become one of twin souls, growing together on deeper levels. Some seemingly simple people achieve a twinship which continues. Others may start believing in their twinship and fall apart. It's all part of *soul* experience—not sex. Some badly hurt and separated on earth can discover later the twinship that was there.

You used to say, Pop, that those whose marriage

service you were taking were standing before you because of something real that had brought them there, and you used to ask them to remember this and hold on to it. That is often very, very true, but human beings can be so very wilful and very blind. Out of holding on can come a twinship that lasts.

There's a difference between the idea of twinship with another which is really a meeting on a deeper level of two souls (not necessarily always the same two perhaps) and the association of a larger number in a group. Of course, the group is closely attuned and pursuing similar aims and ends, but within the group are some more closely attuned to each other than the other group members.

I, on earth, knew several to whom I felt drawn and attuned to a degree, but there was all the difference in the world when I saw Pop or Mum approaching. This does not mean there weren't times when I was off beam with Mum and Pop and more on beam with others. But there still remained that basic ground of being you think of as twinship.

It's quite possible for what I understand as a twin soul to be a guide, e.g., you could say Pop as my twin soul was my guide on earth. In some ways he still is. Equally you could say I'm a bit of a guide now to him. We do meet on deep levels often now. Here we rather lose sight of terms like twin—it's the meeting we find significant.

Is the physical universe bounded or not?

I cannot answer that. If I could I would be presumably as great as the mind of God. I'm just as much a part of the ongoing process as you are. I haven't *all* the answers. I doubt if anyone has. Certainly common spatial notions are far too limited, but the way you have developed your question raises mighty issues. Wasn't there a hymn that the Lord hath yet more light and truth to break forth from his word? None of us—at least as far as I've got—knows the world complete and entire. I can only say that to me it all appears *boundless*.

Men create their own forms, images, organisations, structures, to carry the spiritual truths and visions they seek. They make, in the process, some very bad, though very human mistakes. They make prisons of their own perceptions very often. True and full spiritual consciousness is not limited to any one part of the universe. It is *there* always and everywhere, *there* to be reached, touched, felt, experienced in a myriad ways. Man makes the forms.

Ideas, like all evolving things, cannot be contained in language, or expressed adequately. It's hard when you're part of an ever-growing process to show an end product, for the end product is itself neither in sight nor entirely understood. Can you understand a new quality of awareness lifted out of earth's usual evaluations? When you're above, beyond, you leave behind so much that has seemed important before—even one's earlier highest aims and values can appear dwarfed. If that is true for folk like me, how much more must it be true for the great ones?

Chapter 9

POSTLUDE

WHAT have you been mainly trying to pass on through these talks?

I wanted to convey my experience and findings. The majority of those on your side who pursue this quest via psychical studies often make mistakes or they misinterpret genuine communications from our side. They need a much wider vision and freer approach with the eye of the poet-scientist. It's too easy for them to get bogged down in old forms, particularly when the wider and keener vision is there to be seen with just, so to say, a turn of the head. By turning the head I mean a more constant merging or joining of the poet's insight and vision with the scientists's logic and care. It seemed to me I might be able to challenge folk to look deeper, and to bring a widening of the aspects touched on—an opening up, a sharing with other seeking minds.